"For Such a Time as This"

Steva Harrod

"For Such a Time as This"

ISBN: Softcover

Copyright © 2023 by Steva Harrod

All scripture is from The King James Version.

Parson's Porch Books is an imprint of Parson's Porch *&* Company (PP*&*C) in Cleveland, Tennessee. PP*&*C is a self-funded charity which earns money by publishing books of noted authors, representing all genres. Its face and voice is **David Russell Tullock** who you can contact at: dtullock@parsonsporch.com.

Parson's Porch *&* Company *turns books into bread & milk* by sharing its profits with the poor.

www.parsonsporch.com

"For Such a Time as This"

Contents

TO MOM AND DAD,

perfectly placed in time

God's Wide-Angle Lens

My Dad was into photography in a big way throughout most of his life, even working part-time during college as a photographer for a large city's newspaper. He enjoyed the technical parts of photography and always had a fancy camera or two at home. In his later years, he kept a nice camera in his Jeep just for those occasions when he discovered a picture in the making. A local policeman saw Dad standing on top of his Jeep with a large camera in his hands early one morning in our small downtown area. After asking Dad if he needed help, Dad explained that the early morning sunlight was perfectly positioned for a picture of one of the local churches. Dad snapped several shots, using a variety of angles while balancing himself on top of his vehicle.

The policeman stayed right there until Dad had made his way back down to the pavement.

We take pictures of those moments in time that we want to preserve, those specific quick snapshots of life: a person, a building, a performance, or nature putting on a show. The wide-angle lens is capable of exaggerating perspective in order to include more elements of the setting. The wide-angle lens can obtain an increased depth of field, making it easier to have everything both close and far away in sharp focus, thus filling the frame, making a photographer's dream shot. (I credit the internet for all of that wide-angle lens information.)

God's wide-angle lens is capable of doing what today's cameras can do - and so, so much more. We capture isolated moments in time. God's wide-angle lens captures thousands of years of singular moments, revealing the impacts of individuals' lives throughout time, highlighting the critical moments of trust, faith, and acting on God's leading. Many of those moments in time are pictured in one of God's albums called The Old Testament. Each of those moments had specific people, born for that moment, fulfilling God's purpose. Noah, Abraham and Sarah, Moses, Joseph, Rahab, Samson, Ruth and Naomi, Queen Esther, David and every single Bible character - all born "for such a time as this".

Trusting God in all things, praying in all things, knowing that God's perfect will for our lives may include beautiful, and not so beautiful, isolated moments, allows us to experience the joy and peace of knowing that He is creating the elements of His wide-angle lens picture for our lives now and His forever story.

"...and who knoweth whether thou art come to the kingdom for such a time as this?" Esther 4:14

God's Flood

"And it repented the Lord that he had made man on the earth, and it grieved him at his heart. And the Lord said, I will destroy man whom I have created from the face of the earth; both man, and beast, and the creeping thing, and the fowls of the air; for it repented me that I have made them. But Noah found grace in the eyes of the Lord." Genesis 6:6-8

The recent lockdowns experienced during the Covid pandemic brought to light the seriousness of isolation and our ability to remain emotionally, physically, and mentally healthy while following recommended protocols. During this period of time, I often thought of the story of Noah, and I spent time in the book of Genesis refreshing my mind of this major story that was such a favorite as a child. Noah was enduring a pandemic of wickedness all around him. He loved and trusted God when all else around him was evil.

God was sickened by the evil, wicked behaviors of man, and he decided to destroy mankind with a flood, but "Noah was a just man and perfect in his generations, and Noah walked with God."

The remainder of chapter six relates the goodness of Noah, the corruption of man, and God's detailed blueprints for the building of the ark. Noah and his three sons are tasked with building this massive ark which will be their home for several months, along with many animals.

Noah's physical and emotional strengths were key attributes as he worked daily, along with his sons. His wife and his sons' wives were baking loaf after loaf of bread, gathering herbs and other plants, vegetables, fruit, and fresh water to store in the ark for an unknown length of time. I imagine Noah's neighbors were talking about him non-stop as all of this activity was taking place. Keep in mind that Noah was six hundred years old when the flood was on the earth, so he's quite the older man tackling this project.

Noah persevered, and finally the day came when he, his wife, and their three sons with their wives entered the ark. Next, God leads the animals to enter the ark, and then, "the Lord shut him in." Genesis 7:16

The Bible tells us that seven days later, "the fountains of the great deep were broken up and the heavens were opened. And the rain was upon the earth for forty days and forty nights." When I was a young girl in Sunday School, that forty days of rain stuck with me, but I don't ever remember being told about the seven days prior to the flood beginning. If there had been a daily newspaper or internet news feed in Noah's time, what would those outside of the ark have written during those seven days when not a raindrop could be found? Social media would be in a frenzy about the animals and family inside a giant ark. Then, the earth and the heavens opened. Water. The animals and Noah's family can hear the water hitting the ark's roof and feel the ark beginning to respond to the surging water rising from inside the earth.

Soon, the ark might have begun to rock a bit in the growing depths of the water. The inhabitants of the land weren't laughing anymore. Maybe some were trying to make Noah hear them, trying to gain access inside the ark. Noah had preached and talked to people for years about trusting God, and the Bible tells us not one person believed.

"All in whose nostrils was the breath of life, of all that was in the dry land, died." Genesis 7:22

I've often wondered just how many miracles God performed inside that ark during those many months of isolation. Feeding and caring for the animals consumed much of the family's time. Taking care of one another was important, too. Those eight people had to be a team. We will have an eternity to ask Noah questions and to listen to his stories.

Noah was the team leader inside that ark, and my imagination sees a strong man giving encouragement as he gives instructions. Noah trusted God.

Forty days and nights of water from inside the earth and from the heavens above were followed by one hundred, fifty days of waiting for the water to flow into the sea or to evaporate. Chapter eight states that after ten months inside the ark, Noah saw the tops of the mountains. The ark was resting "upon the mountains of Ararat." After several more weeks, "Noah removed the covering of the ark, and looked, and behold, the face of the ground was dry."

No long pandemic walks, no runs around the neighborhood, no yard work, no cross-country skiing on the local trails, no internet shopping, or no New York Times word games for those eight people. Close to a year inside the ark with one another and all of those animals!

God told Noah to let down the ark's door, allowing all of the animals and his family to walk on dry ground again. Noah built an offering to God in thanksgiving for His goodness.

God told Noah's three sons and their three wives to replenish the earth.

Genesis tells us that Noah became a farmer, tending the land and his family for the remainder of his years. He lived another three hundred, fifty years after leaving the ark, trusting in the God of his salvation.

"And all the days of Noah were nine hundred, fifty years: and he died." Genesis 9:28-29 "By faith Noah, being warned of God of things not seen as yet, moved with fear, prepared an ark to the saving of his house; by the which he condemned the world, and became heir of the righteousness which is by faith." Hebrews 11:7

Abraham

"Now faith is the substance of things hoped for, the evidence of things not seen." Hebrews 11:1

"And the scripture was fulfilled which saith, Abraham believed God, and it was imputed unto him for righteousness: and he was called the Friend of God." James 2:23

ABRAHAM. The name brings courage and strength to mind.

Abraham's belief and trust in God resulted in obedience to God. All throughout the Bible, Abraham is recognized for his responses to God's guidance.

The birth of Isaac fulfilled God's proclamation to Abraham that he would become a father of nations. Abraham, Isaac, Jacob, and then Jacob's twelve sons were the beginnings of the

Israelite nation, with each of these men having pivotal parts in the progression of history.

Strength of character, respect, reverence, obedience, unwavering faith and trust are the building blocks of the man, Abraham. I am only using scripture to highlight Abraham's life.

"Now these are the generations of Terah: Terah begat Abram, Nahor, and Haran, and Haran begat Lot.

And Haran died before his father Terah in the land of his nativity, in Ur of the Chaldees.

And Abram and Nahor took them wives: the name of Abram's wife was Sarai; and the name of Nahor's wife, Milcah, the daughter of Haran, the father of Milcah, and the father of Iscah.

But Sarai was barren; she had no child."
Genesis 11:27-30

"After these things the word of the Lord came unto Abram in a vision, saying, Fear not, Abram: I am thy shield, and thy exceeding great reward.

He that shall come forth out of thine own bowels shall be thine heir.

And he brought him forth abroad, and said, Look now toward heaven, and tell the stars, if thou be able to number them: and he said unto him, So shall thy seed be.

And he believed in the Lord; and he counted it to him for righteousness.

And he said unto him, I am the Lord that brought thee out of Ur of the Chaldees, to give thee this land to inherit it."

And he said unto Abram, Know of a surety that thy seed shall be a stranger in a land that is not theirs, and shall serve them; and they shall afflict them four hundred years.

And also that nation, whom they shall serve, will I judge and afterward shall they come out with great substance.

In the same day the Lord made a covenant with Abram, saying, Unto thy seed have I given this land, from the river of Egypt unto the great river, the river Euphrates." Genesis 15:1, 4-7, 13-14, 18

"And when Abram was ninety years old and nine, the Lord appeared to Abram, and said unto him, I am the Almighty God; walk before me, and be thou perfect.

And I will make my covenant between me and thee and will multiply thee exceedingly.

And Abram fell on his face: and God talked with him, saying,

As for me, behold, my covenant is with thee, and thou shalt be a father of many nations.

Neither shall thy name any more be called Abram, but thy name shall be Abraham; for a father of many nations have I made thee.

And I will make thee exceeding fruitful, and I will make nations of thee, and kings shall come out of thee.

And I will establish my covenant between me and thee and thy seed after thee in their generations for an everlasting covenant, to be a God unto thee, and to thy seed after thee.

And I will give unto thee, and to thy seed after thee, the land wherein thou art a stranger, all the land of Canaan, for an everlasting possession; and I will be their God." Genesis 17:1-8

"And the Lord visited Sarah as he had said, and the Lord did unto Sarah as he had spoken.

For Sarah conceived, and bare Abraham a son in his old age, at the set time of which God had spoken to him.

And Abraham called the name of his son that was born unto him, whom Sarah bare to him, Isaac.

And Abraham circumcised his son Isaac being eight days old, as God had commanded him.

And Abraham was an hundred years old when his son Isaac was born unto him.

And Sarah said, God hath made me to laugh, so that all that hear will laugh with me.

And she said, Who would have said unto Abraham, that Sarah should have given children suck? for I have given him a son in his old age.

And the child grew and was weaned: and Abraham made a great feast the same day that Isaac was weaned." Genesis 21:1-8

"And it came to pass after these things, that God did tempt Abraham, and said unto him, Abraham: and he said, Behold, here I am.

And he said, Take now thy son, thine only son Isaac, whom thou lovest, and get thee into the land of Moriah; and offer him there for a burnt offering upon one of the mountains which I will tell thee of.

And Abraham rose up early in the morning, and saddled his ass, and took two of his young men with him, and Isaac his son, and clave the wood for the burnt-offering, and rose up, and went unto the place of which God had told him.

And Isaac spake unto Abraham his father, and said, My father: and he said, Here am I, my son. And he said, Behold the fire and the wood: but where is the lamb for a burnt offering?

My son, God will provide himself a lamb for a burnt offering: so they went both of them together.

Abraham built an altar, laid the wood in order, and bound Isaac his son, and laid him on the altar upon the wood.

And Abraham stretched forth his hand and took the knife to slay his son.

And the angel of the Lord called unto him out of heaven, and said, Abraham, Abraham: and he said, Here am I.

And he said, Lay not thine hand upon the lad, neither do thou anything unto him: for now I know that you fearest God, seeing thou hast not withheld thy son, thine only son from me.

And Abraham lifted up his eyes, and looked, and behold behind him a ram caught in a thicket by his horns: and Abraham went

and took the ram and offered him up for a burnt offering in the stead of his son.

The angel of the Lord called unto Abraham out of heaven the second time, Saying, By myself have I sworn, saith the Lord, for because thou hast done this thing, and hast not withheld thy son, thine only son:

That in blessing I will bless thee, and in multiplying I will multiply thy seed as the stars of the heaven, and as the sand which is upon the sea shore; and thy seed shall possess the gate of his enemies;

And in thy seed shall all the nations of the earth be blessed; because thou hast obeyed my voice." Genesis 22:1-3, 6-18

"And these are the days of the years of Abraham's life which he lived, an hundred three score and fifteen years.

Then Abraham gave up the ghost, and died in a good old age, an old man, and full of years; and was gathered to his people.

And his sons Isaac and Ishmael buried him in the cave of Machpelah, in the field of Ephron the son of Zohar the Hittite, which is before Mamre;

The field which Abraham purchased of the sons of Heth: there was Abraham buried, and Sarah his wife." Genesis 25:7-10

"That the blessing of Abraham might come on the Gentiles through Jesus Christ; that we might receive the promise of the Spirit through faith.

Now to Abraham and his seed were the promises made. He saith not, And to seeds, as of many; but as of one, And to thy seed, which is Christ.

For if the inheritance be of the law, it is no more of promise: but God gave it to Abraham by promise.

But the scripture hath concluded all under sin, that the promise by faith of Jesus Christ might be given to them that believe.

For you are all the children of God by faith in Christ Jesus.

And if ye be Christ's, then are ye Abraham's seed, and heirs according to the promise."

Galatians 3:14,16,18,22,26,29

"By faith Abraham, when he was called to go out into a place which he should after receiving for an inheritance, obeyed; and he went out, not knowing whither he went.

By faith he sojourned in the land of promise, as in a strange country, dwelling in tabernacles with Isaac and Jacob, the heirs with him of the same promise:

For he looked for a city which hath foundations, whose builder and maker is God.

Through faith also Sarah herself received strength to conceive seed and was delivered of a child when she was past age, because she judged him faithfully who had promised.

Therefore sprang there even of one, and him as good as dead, so many as the stars of the sky in multitude, and as the sand which is by the seashore innumerable.

These all died in faith, not having received the promises, but having seen them afar off, and were persuaded of them, and embraced them, and confessed that they were strangers and pilgrims on the earth.

By faith Abraham, when he was tried, offered up Isaac: and he that had received the promises offered up his only begotten son.

Of whom it was said, That in Isaac shall thy seed be called:

Accounting that God was able to raise him up, even from the dead; from whence also he received him in a figure."

Hebrews 11:8 -13; 17-19

"Was not Abraham our father justified by works, when he had offered Isaac his son upon the altar?

Seest thou how faith wrought with his works, and by works was faith made perfect?

And the scripture was fulfilled which saith, Abraham believed God, and it was imputed unto him for righteousness: and was called the Friend of God."

James 2:21-23

The Battle Of Jericho

" ... for the Lord your God, he is God in heaven above, and in earth beneath." Joshua 2:11

One of my favorite childhood Bible stories is about the seven priests with the seven trumpets made of rams' horns marching around the walled city of Jericho. Singing the final lines of that old chorus, "... and the walls came a tumbling down" was always a Sunday School treat. With age, the story became a small part of a multitude of favorite Old Testament stories.

The Old Testament book of Joshua begins shortly following the death of Moses, the leader of this large group of the Israelite people, the man who spiritually and physically led these thousands of people as they waffled from diligent obedience to loud rebellion several times throughout their journey. In the opening verses of chapter one, God tells Joshua that he is now the chosen leader of the children of Israel, also giving Joshua firm declarations of His abiding presence. There are battles to fight and lands to claim, and God presses the point of His unfailing guidance and presence in verses five through nine. "Have not I commanded thee?

"Be strong and of a good courage; be not afraid, neither be thou dismayed: for the Lord thy God is with thee whithersoever thou goest."

Joshua's first conquest was to be the city of Jericho. He sent two young unnamed spies to view the land and the city. The two spies came into Rahab's house on the wall and lodged there, according to Joshua 2:1. Rahab hides the two spies on the roof, covering them with stalks of flax, but before she covers them, she asks them to promise her that when the Israelite army attacks Jericho, she and her family will be saved. The two spies tell her if she will protect them, the lives of her and her family will be saved before the attack. Soldiers from the king soon arrive at Rahab's door, asking the whereabouts of the two men. Rahab tells them that the two men left the city before dark as the city gates were closing, and she had no idea where they were. She suggests to the guards that if they pursue them now, they should find them quickly. So, the king's men leave the city in pursuit of the spies. Once back up on the roof, she relays the story to the men, telling them to hide in the mountain for three days to give the king's men time to look and return home, which is what they did.

The spies and Rahab devise their escape plan and their plan to notify the Israelite army of the location of her home whenever the battle happens. The same scarlet rope that the spies use to go down the wall from her house will be hung from the window before the battle to alert the army of her location.

Later in chapter six, the battle of Jericho begins with the seven priests marching around the city's walls blowing the trumpets made of rams' horns. They circle the city once each day for six days, and on the seventh day, they circle the city seven times while blowing their trumpets. As the priests begin their seventh lap, Joshua tells the people to begin shouting as the priests walk that seventh lap - and those walls "came a tumbling down."

"By faith the walls of Jericho fell down, after they were compassed about seven days." Hebrews 11:30

Let's back up to the very end of chapter five, verses thirteen through fifteen, to moments prior to the priests beginning that very first lap around the walls. The priests, the people, and Joshua are ready to begin, following God's directions for the seven days of marching around the city when Joshua sees a man close to him with his sword drawn, and he asks him whose side he is on. "As captain of the host of the Lord am I now come. And Joshua fell on his face to the earth and did worship. "What saith my lord unto his servant?" "Loose thy shoe from off thy foot; for the place whereon thou standest is holy." And Joshua did so." Regardless of how many times I've read this story, those three verses give me goosebumps. The captain of the host of God was standing right there, waiting for this battle to begin, ready to fight with the Israelite army to lead them to victory.

Joshua tells the two young spies in Joshua 6:22, "Go into the harlot's house, and bring out the woman, all that she hath, as ye swore unto her."

After Rahab and all of her family and possessions had been safely placed with the Israelite people, Joshua's army killed everyone in Jericho, young and old, and burned their city, taking the silver, the gold, and the vessels of brass and iron for the treasury of the house of the Lord. We learn later that one Israelite stole items from what had been taken, and he and his family were stoned and buried together by Joshua's men.

Rahab's amazing story continues, and we will read of her again both in the Old and New Testaments.

"And Joshua saved Rahab the harlot alive, and her father's household, and all that she had; and she dwelleth in Israel even unto this day; because she hid the messengers, which Joshua sent to spy out Jericho." Joshua 6:25

Samson's Heart

"And the children of Israel did evil again in the sight of the Lord: and the Lord delivered them into the hands of the Philistines forty years." Judges 13:1

"And the woman bare a son and called his name Samson: and the child grew, and the Lord blessed him." Judges 13:24

Samson's story begins with an angel visiting an unnamed Israelite woman. The angel tells this woman, who was barren, that she is going to conceive a son. The angel continues speaking to her, giving her direct instructions about what she is to eat and drink during her pregnancy, and then adds that she is never to cut her son's hair. "For the child shall be a Nazarite unto God from the womb: and he shall begin to deliver Israel out of the hand of the Philistines." Judges 13:5 Samson's purpose for his life is clear from the very beginning.

The woman goes home to her husband, Manoah, and tells him of the angel's visit. A few days later, the angel visits the woman again, and she immediately runs home to tell Manoah to go with her to meet the angel. Manoah asks the angel if what his wife told him about them having a son is true, and the angel repeats to Manoah all that he said to the woman during his first visit with her.

The writer of the book of Judges jumps from Samson's birth to Samson as a young man. We read the stories of the Spirit of the Lord coming upon Samson, giving him phenomenal physical strength. Samson killed a lion with his bare hands and slew one thousand Philistines with the jawbone of an ass.

Samson became a judge of the Israelite people and remained a judge for twenty years.

Yet, as with all of us, Samson wasn't perfect. He worshiped God, loved God, and trusted God. He knew God was the source of his abilities and that God had placed him on earth at this specific time for a special purpose. However, Samson was a man with strong appetites, and those appetites led to trouble.

Samson's attraction to beautiful women was his weakest trait. The writer of Judges tells us stories of Samson's desires, the final beautiful woman in his story being Delilah, a woman the Bible tells us Samson loved.

A group of Philistine lords approached Delilah with a deal to betray Samson. If she could discover from Samson what gave him his extraordinary physical strength and then share that discovery with them, they would pay her eleven hundred pieces of silver. She agreed to the deal and began trying to trick Samson into revealing the truth about his strength. Samson didn't give her the truth until Delilah said, "How can you say you love me if you don't answer me truthfully?" Samson finally said, "There hath not come a razor upon mine head. If I be shaven, then my strength will go from me, and I shall become weak."

Samson falls asleep on Delilah's knees. She beckons a man to come into their room to shave his head, and then she awakens him with the words, "The Philistines be upon you, Samson." Samson awakens to discover his strength has left him. The Philistines bound him, gouged out his eyes, and took him to prison.

"Howbeit the hair of his head began to grow again after he was shaven."

Time passes, and the Philistines are having a victory celebration in a large building. During the party, some of the Philistines suggest bringing Samson out of his prison cell to make a mockery of him. A young boy is asked to bring Samson to them. Amidst the jeering and the laughter of the large crowd of people, the boy and Samson arrived inside the building.

Samson knew what he had to do, and he asked the boy for his help. The boy guided Samson's hands to the two middle pillars holding up the house. Then, Samson prayed this prayer: "O Lord God, remember me, I pray thee, and strengthen me, I pray thee, only this once, O God, that I may be at once avenged of the Philistines for my two eyes."

Samson's gifted strength returns to his body, and he is able to bring down the roof of that building, killing the three thousand Philistines who were attending the party, beginning the deliverance of the Israelites from the Philistine's power, just as the angel had shared with his parents years earlier.

The book of Judges tells us that Samson's family took his body and buried Samson in the burying place of Manoah, his father.

"And what more shall I say? for the time would fail me to tell of Gideon, and of Barak, and of Samson, and of Jepthae, of David also, and Samuel, and of the prophets: Who through faith subdued kingdoms, wrought righteousness, obtained promises, stopped the mouths of lions..." Hebrews 11:32-33

"Amazing grace, how sweet the sound, That saved a wretch like me!

I once was lost, but now am found; Was blind, but now I see.

Through many dangers, toils, and snares, I have already come;

'Tis grace hath brought me safe this far, And grace will lead me home."

John Newton, 1722

Naomi and Ruth

The Old Testament contains several stories
about famine, resulting in families packing their
lives and moving to a different area for
survival, and in the book of Ruth, we find one
of those stories. This book is only four
chapters in length, yet those chapters are
packed with pictures for us of what life was like
in Israel during B.C. 1322-1312.

"Now it came to pass in the days when the
judges ruled, that there was a famine in the
land. And a certain man of Bethlehem-Judah
went to sojourn in the country of Moab, he,
and his wife, and his two sons." Ruth 1:1

Elimelech, Naomi, and their two sons left
their Bethlehem home and walked thirty
miles or so to Moab to escape the famine.
Once there, life began happening fast for this
family of four. Soon after their arrival in their

new town, Elimelech dies. Next, the two sons fell in love with two girls from Moab, Ruth and Orpah, and married them. Then, the two sons died, leaving Naomi alone, save for her daughters-in-law.

Naomi decides to return to her Bethlehem home, and the two young women begin the long walk with her, but Naomi tells them to return to the homes of their mothers to begin anew. The three women are crying, knowing that Naomi's choice to return home is the right one, but they will miss her. Orpah turns, walking back to Moab to her mother's home. Ruth clings to Naomi, saying those very famous verses to her.

"And Ruth said, entreat me not to leave thee, or to return from following after thee: for whither thou goest, I will go; and where thou lodgest, I will lodge: thy people shall be my people, and thy God my God:

Where thou diest, will I die, and there will I be buried: the Lord do so to me, and more also, if ought but death part thee and me." Ruth 1:16-17

Ruth's respect and love for Naomi is providing physical and emotional support for Naomi as they begin the journey to Bethlehem together.

"So Naomi returned, and Ruth the Moabitess, her daughter-in-law, with her, which returned out of the country of Moab: and they came to Bethlehem in the beginning of barley harvest." Ruth 1:22

The saying, "Timing is everything," certainly applies here. Barley harvest is happening, and Naomi's kinsman of her husband's family, Boaz, is busy in the fields with his workers. Naomi can't stop herself from playing matchmaker, and she creates a plan to make sure Ruth is in the fields when Boaz is also there. Boaz is a "mighty man of wealth", and also a kind, generous man.

Ruth and Boaz meet a few times, becoming acquainted with each other. He purchased the remaining properties of Elimelech and Naomi's two sons, and he took Ruth to be his wife.

Ruth and Boaz have a son, Obed, who would later become King David's grandfather.

This story offers another amazingly spectacular detail in God's wide-angle lens picture: Boaz's mother is none other than Rahab from the first three chapters of Joshua! Matthew 1:5 tells us that Rahab met and married Salmon after escaping Jericho with her family. Rahab and Salmon's son was Boaz. Rahab was King David's great, great grandmother.

"By faith, the harlot Rahab perished not with them that believed not, when she had received the spies with peace." Hebrews 11:31

Samuel, Saul, and David

"The book of the generation of Jesus Christ, the son of David, the son of Abraham." Matthew 1:1

"And when God had removed Saul, He raised up unto them David to be their king: to whom also He gave testimony, and said, I have found David the son of Jesse, a man after mine own heart, which shall fulfill all my will.

Of this man's seed hath God according to His promise raised unto Israel a Savior, Jesus." Acts 13:22-23

The first mention of David in the Bible is found in Ruth 4:22:

"And Obed begat Jesse, and Jesse begat David." Boaz and Ruth, the parents of Obed, were the great-grandparents of David.

Paul tells us in Act 13 a brief history of the Israelite people, leading to God choosing David as the second king of Israel. We read that this nation of people were led by judges for approximately four hundred and fifty years with Samuel being the last judge. The people pleaded with Samuel for a king after Samuel had appointed his sons judges over Israel. Samuel wasn't happy about what was taking place, and "Samuel prayed unto the Lord." 1 Samuel 8:6

Several verses later we read: "And the Lord said to Samuel, Hearken unto their voice, and make them a king." God leads Samuel to Saul, and soon thereafter, Samuel anoints Saul as king. Samuel's heart is heavy with sadness as he has watched the Israelites turn away from God's leading, instead wanting to live as other nations do. Samuel prepares a proclamation to deliver to the people as Saul becomes the first king of Israel. The last two verses of the proclamation: "Only fear the Lord and serve him in truth with all your heart: for consider how great things he hath done for you. But if ye shall still do wickedly, ye shall be consumed, both ye and your king."

The book of 1Samuel is a detailed history lesson of the Israelite nation as Samuel, their highly respected judge and Godly leader, grows old and the people demand change. King Saul becomes overwhelmed by his own strong self-will, and wanting to please the people, he disobeys God. Power seems to feed his soul, leading to jealousy and unstable emotions. Serving God with all his heart isn't happening, and major trouble is looming.

Saul disobeys God's directions during a battle, and Samuel is sickened with sadness by Saul's actions. God tells Samuel to go to Bethlehem to meet Jesse. Samuel is afraid of Saul's anger, and God tells him not to fear, that He will tell him what to do and what to say. As 1Samuel 16 unfolds, God closely leads Samuel to Jesse's home, meets seven of his sons, and God says, "No, not these men." Samuel asks Jesse if he has more sons. "There's one more keeping the sheep." "Send for him." Two verses later, Samuel is anointing David the next king of Israel. "And the Spirit of the Lord came upon David from that day forward."

The story of David is more than a slingshot taking down an ego driven Philistine giant, more than David being the youngest of eight sons of Jesse, more than David being a very strong shepherd boy who killed a lion and a bear while protecting his flock of sheep, more than a boy who was a gifted musician. Putting all of those qualities and many more together gives us a picture of this boy the Bible called "ruddy, with a beautiful countenance, and goodly to look to."

Saul and David's story has many twists and turns, with Saul's jealousy of David bringing about attempts on David's life. Samuel's death happens shortly before Saul, his three sons, and much of his army are killed in battle with the Philistines.

David's heart was filled with gratitude for all that God had done for him and through him for the Israelite nation. We have his Psalms of prayer and praise, revealing David's soul. Was he a perfect man?

No. David's closeness to God resulted in a repenting spirit, in crying out to God for forgiveness, and also in shouting praises for God's goodness, glory, and grace.

"The LORD is my rock, and my fortress, and my deliverer; The God of my rock: in Him will I trust; he is my shield, and the horn of my salvation, my high tower, and my refuge, my savior; thou savest me from violence.

I will call on the LORD, who is worthy to be praised: so shall I be saved from mine enemies." 11 Samuel 22:2-4

"But let all those that put their trust in thee rejoice, let them ever shout for joy, because thou defendest them: let them also that love thy name be joyful in thee." Psalm 5:11

"For with thee is the fountain of life: in thy light shall we see light." Psalm 36:9

"Cause me to hear thy lovingkindness in the morning; for in thee do I trust, cause me to know the way wherein I should walk; for I lift up my soul unto thee." Psalm 143:8

"Let everything that hath breath praise the LORD. Praise ye the LORD." Psalm 150:6

King David's Closing Prayer of Praise

"Thine, O Lord, is the greatness, and the power, and the glory, and the victory, and the majesty: for all that is in the heaven and in the earth is thine; thine is the kingdom, O LORD, and thou are exalted as head above all." 1 Chronicles 29:11

King David's Prayer of Thanksgiving

1 CHRONICLES 28 - 29

King David gathered his congregation, telling them that his heart's plan was to build a new temple for the Ark of the Covenant, but God had instead told him the job would go to his son, Solomon, because David had been a "man of war, and had shed blood." David continued sharing from his heart, saying that God had chosen Solomon to now become the next king, "to sit upon the throne of the kingdom of the LORD over Israel."

28:9 - "And thou, Solomon my son, know thou the God of thy father, and serve him with a perfect heart and with a willing mind: for the LORD searcheth all hearts, and understandeth all the imaginations of the thoughts: if thou seek him, he will be found of thee; but if thou forsake him, he will cast thee off forever. 10 - Take heed now; for the LORD hath chosen thee to build an house for the sanctuary: be strong and do it." 20 - "And David said to Solomon his son, Be strong and of good courage, and do it: fear not, nor be dismayed: for the LORD God, even my God, will be with thee; he will not fail thee, nor forsake thee, until thou hast finished all the work for the service of the house of the LORD."

King David keeps talking, sharing what he has personally given for the building of the new temple and encouraging the congregation to make their own offerings. Chapter 29 tells us that the people "willingly" made their gifts, "and David the king also rejoiced with great joy."

The tone of these two chapters seems filled with David sensing his end-of-life period is beginning, and he is wanting to encourage, guide, and send his people into a new era keeping God as their ultimate leader.

David's prayer in verses twelve through nineteen of chapter twenty-nine is a favorite prayer and passage of many people, including me.

"Both riches and honor come of thee, and thou reignest over all; and in thine hand is power and might; and in thine hand it is to make great, and to give strength unto all.

Now therefore, our God, we thank thee, and praise thy glorious name.

But who am I, and what is my people, that we should be able to offer so willingly after this sort? for all things come of thee, and of thine own have we given thee.

For we are strangers before thee, and sojourners, as were all our fathers: our days on the earth are as a shadow, and there is none abiding.

O LORD our God, all this store that we have prepared to build thee an house for thine holy name cometh of thine hand and is all thine own.

I know also, my God, that thou triest the heart, and hast pleasure in uprightness. As for me, in the uprightness of my heart I have willingly offered all these things: and now have I seen with joy thy people, which are present here, to offer willingly unto thee.

O LORD God of Abraham, Isaac, and of Israel, our fathers, keep this forever in the imagination of the thoughts of the heart of thy people, and prepare their heart unto thee.

And give unto Solomon my son a perfect heart, to keep thy commandments, thy testimonies, and thy statutes, and to do all these things, and to build the palace, for the which I have made provision."

David's words in these two chapters reveal his thankfulness to God for all that God has provided to him and to his people and his belief that everything we have and are is from God.

David knows as he speaks on this day that he will soon be stepping down as king, and Solomon will receive the position.

The final verses of 1 Chronicles memorialize David's life and reign over Israel.

"Thus David the son of Jesse reigned over all Israel.

And the time that he reigned over Israel was forty years...

And he died in a good old age, full of days, riches, and honor, and Solomon his son reigned in his stead."

Jonah

"Jesus answered and said unto them, An evil and adulterous generation seeketh after a sign; and there shall no sign be given to it, but the sign of the prophet Jonas:

For as Jonas was three days and three nights in the whale's belly; so shall the Son of man be three days and three nights in the heart of the earth.

The men of Nineveh shall rise in judgement with this generation and shall condemn it: because they repented at the preaching of Jonas; and behold, a greater than Jonas is here."
Matthew 12:39-41

"Now the word of the Lord came unto Jonah the son of Amittai, saying,

"Arise, go to Nineveh, that great city, and cry against it; for their wickedness is come up before me."

But, Jonah rose up to flee unto Tarshish from the presence of the Lord and went down to Joppa; and he found a ship going to Tarshish: so he paid the fare thereof, and went down into it, to go with them unto Tarshish from the presence of the Lord." Jonah 1:1-3

We are obviously not given the psychological profile of Jonah in these three opening verses of the book of Jonah, but the man is unsettled enough to put on his running shoes to attempt to flee from God's presence. Jonah soon learns that trying to run from God isn't a wise choice. God had told Jonah to go to Nineveh to preach to the people about forsaking their evil choices and turn to God for repentance and new choices.

Jonah's heart was filled with belief in God, but he apparently was upset that God's mercy was reaching down to such a wicked people. Or, maybe he was afraid of what the people would do to him as he preached God's message of "Yet forty days, and Nineveh shall be overthrown." Jonah knew all of the worldly risks of going to this land. He became overwhelmed with anger, fear, and maybe even a lack of trust in God's care.

What a journal entry we have been given in those four chapters of Jonah! Jonah buys a ticket for passage on a sailboat to Tarshish, goes down into the boat "and he lay, and was fast asleep."

God acts quickly in this story, causing the winds to become "tempestuous against them." The sailors rowed hard to attempt to overcome the strength of the storm, but all of their efforts were to no avail. They cried out to God to forgive them for what they were about to do; they threw Jonah overboard, "and the sea immediately ceased from her raging." The sailors again began their prayers to God.

"Now the Lord had prepared a great fish to swallow up Jonah. And Jonah was in the belly of the fish three days and three nights." Jonah 1:17

I've never been swallowed by an actual whale, but I have experienced the sickening feeling of knowing I was out of God's will for my life. Those "in the belly of the whale" moments are moments of physical and emotional turmoil, spiritual repentance, followed with renewal, moments of freshness, and moments of knowing God's grace and love.

"For thou hadst cast me into the deep, in the midst of the seas; and the floods compassed me about: all thy billows and thy waves passed over me.

Then I said, I am cast out of thy sight; yet I will look again toward thy holy temple.

But I will sacrifice unto thee with the voice of thanksgiving; I will pay that that I have vowed. Salvation is of the Lord."

"And the Lord spake unto the fish, and it vomited out Jonah upon the dry land." Jonah 2:3-4, 9-10

Chapter three tells the details of Jonah's words to Nineveh and the people's quick repentance, including that of their king. God saw how they repented, and He chose not to do any of what he had said he was going to do to their land and people. Jonah becomes upset again when God extends love and grace to the people following the historical revival he had witnessed through his preaching. Even after experiencing God forgiving him for running away to Tarshish instead of immediately going to Nineveh, Jonah is again harboring anger toward God for forgiving Nineveh so quickly. He can't let it go.

Remember the parable of The Prodigal Son in Luke 15:11? The father divides his legacy between his two sons. The older son stays and continues to work daily in the fields to see to the success of the land. The younger son takes his inheritance with him as he leaves his family, squandering away his money to the point that he is living with the pigs. He returns home, and his father is joyfully planning a celebration for his lost son who is now back at home and sorrowful for his choices. The other son can't understand his father's joy at all. "Don't you see? He has returned home to be with us. Let us rejoice. Son, thou art ever with me, and all that I have is thine. Thy brother was dead, and is alive again; and was lost, and is found." Luke 15: 31-32

Jonah reminds me of the older brother in this parable of Jesus. Jonah, the gifted preacher of God's message, is witnessing in this story the magnitude of God's forgiveness and grace. He experienced forgiveness and grace firsthand, and yet, is again perplexed. We see God's patience as the book of Jonah ends.

"For thou, Lord, art good, and ready to forgive; and plenteous in mercy unto all of them that call upon thee." Psalm 86:5

Thankful

The historical stories of the Old Testament provide us with pictures of beautiful beginnings, viral wickedness, ego tripping power, and passionate love. God's impeccable timing and grace weres working through each person and each situation in powerful, miraculous ways. God's timeline is ongoing, building detail upon detail in the isolated moments of life, His story, our history, those moments when lives are changed, and life is forever altered. His wide-angle lens continues.